# The Art of Fundraising

## The Appeal The People The Strategies

### *REVISED AND EXPANDED*

*by Gary Phillips*

# Table of Contents

# Preface

Last year donors gave over $350 million to more than two million non-profit organizations throughout the United States. Organizations with combined revenues approaching $1 trillion. According to Independent Sector research 44 percent, or over 80 million people throughout our nation volunteer for non-profit organizations each year.

These numbers represent enormous investments of resources and time in our country's non-profit sector. The challenge for any non-profit organization is to be properly positioned to compete effectively for available volunteer time and charitable resources.

My objective in publishing and then updating this book is provide professionals and volunteers alike with often overlooked techniques and field-tested strategies that will help them become more effective fundraising. Help them compete successfully for peoples' time, attention and resources.

If you have found helpful thoughts and suggestions in this book, or you have some suggestions for topics you would like me to address, I will welcome hearing from you:

**Gary Phillips**
contact@phillipsontheweb.com

# About the Author

Gary Phillips is Chairman and Founder of Phillips & Associates, a firm that specializes in strategic and organizational planning, leadership and fundraising counsel exclusively for non-profit organizations. Since 1971, Gary and his firm have helped over 575 organizations raise and manage over $3.7 Billion in funds to improve quality of life in communities throughout the United States through the arts, education, health care, and community services. Prior to forming Phillips & Associates, Gary served as Executive Director of both a private and corporate philanthropic foundation, Director of Development at UCLA, and Assistant Director of Development at Stanford University.

# Acknowledgements

I have had the great good fortune of developing a professional career in philanthropy. Not initially planned but continually prompted by people. People I have worked with, and learned from. People whose lives have been touched and benefited by the organizations I have worked with. People who come to me for professional advice and career guidance. My sincere thanks to all, with special "shout outs" to my colleagues Shelley and Michelle.

# Dedication Page

Most people who consider themselves successful recognize there is someone special who gave them boosts along the way. A thoughtful listener. A compassionate partner. An unabashed cheerleader. For over 55 years, my wife Maileen.

# Introduction:

## Key Elements of a Successful Fundraising Program

Over the years I have developed a useful approach to both developing and examining comprehensive and successful fundraising programs within three basis areas: *The Appeal, The People and The Strategies.*

## *THE APPEAL*

**Financial Planning** - Detailing the organization's current, near-term and long-term funding requirements focusing on:

o   *annual operating costs*

o   *special projects and programs*

o   *major physical plant expansion and renovation*

**Charitable Funding Opportunities** - Identifying from results of financial planning the organization's priority funding needs which will most likely attract private contribution and grant support.

**Case Statement** - Describing the organization's distinctive merit and need for seeking gifts and grants, and articulating the most compelling reasons why someone should consider contributing to meet the represented funding needs.

**Donor/Volunteer Recognition** - Developing the most appropriate methods to acknowledge and recognize donors and volunteers whose gifts and involvement helped meet the represented funding needs.

## THE PEOPLE

**Volunteer Leadership** - Defining and assigning specific roles and responsibilities for volunteer leadership, with particular emphasis on the role of the governing board.

**Potential Donors** - Identifying individuals, foundations, businesses, and charitable associations as potential donors; evaluating their contribution potential; and, assessing the best approach to cultivate and solicit their support.

**Professional Staff** - Employing a sufficient level of professional staff talent, time and expertise to plan and manage the fundraising program.

## THE STRATEGIES

Gathering together the essential elements of a compelling appeal, and connecting with people to communicate the appeal is the basic foundation of fundraising. It is the strategic application of these key elements that make the difference between fundraising and successful fundraising. And not to be overlooked in developing effective fundraising strategies is the logistical support: budgeted financial and material resources; sound administrative policies and systems; effective data base management of donor and constituent records.

*(handwritten notes)*

" 2nd Chance Company
Second Chance Partners

Workforce
~ S.C.P '

Story = s:   Steven King   Taylor
              Carlos        Rob
              Ryan , etc    Shane
              Jorge    Jane J.
          → Chad Keller   James H.

Connected the act of
one human being to
another.

# THE APPEAL

*LA
Cost
70,00*

*↓ 1.4 million-
nonprofit*

Fundraising is a very competitive undertaking. Throughout the United States, there are over 1.4 million non-profit organizations vying for peoples' time, attention and resources. To be successful in fundraising requires keen understandings of what encourages people to be charitable, and a discernment of ways to then motivate their support.

*Impact — changing a person's Life*

*MAKE THAT CONNECTION*

*I, ~~Gary Throne~~ Sarah Switzer, put a set of teeth in Stee King's jaws.*

*I, Yvonne Beardsworth, help Jane H. get into USC School of Journalism*

*I, Bruce Voss, help Oxygn Brandon's Record and set him free.*

"Loud & Proud" about Beau. How
what are we proud of?

- New Life
- Respect in Family
- Career / Money / Business

# Art of Engagement

Most non–profit organizations eventually (and often reluctantly) come face–to–face with what I consider to be the single most important reality of fundraising: *"In order to secure meaningful gifts, we need to engage potential donors in meaningful conversations."*

An obstacle is that most people, however generous with their own time and financial resources, are reluctant to "impose" on others to contribute even to the most worthy organizations and causes. Every person in a leadership position – volunteer or staff – should be expected to engage people in meaningful conversations about their organization, to speak "loud and proud" about its programs, plans and most importantly the people it serves. I have found that most donors expect this level of engagement and are often puzzled by the lack of enthusiastic endorsement from those closest to the organization.

The fact is that effective fundraising is not the art of asking; it's the art of engagement. And both volunteers and staff are more likely to master that art if they share certain key perspectives; for example:

*"We're always looking for opportunities to engage potential donors in meaningful conversations about our organization."*

*"It's important to listen carefully to a potential donor. Their expressed interests and concerns undoubtedly will have a bearing on their eventual support of our organization."*

*"Potential donors expect us to prioritize our funding needs which reflects our overall financial planning."*

*"We only ask for a gift consideration when we feel the potential donor has been well-prepared to give a thoughtful response."*

\* \* \*

**Can you make these statements about your organization's engagement with potential donors?**

# Four Key Questions

In my experience, potential donors have four basic questions in mind, whether spoken or unspoken:

> *"Why should I give anything, at any time, to your organization?"*

> *"What will your organization be able to do more of.... or do better....or avoid the risk of eliminating....as a result of my gift?"*

> *"Who will be better served if I help you meet your fundraising goals?"*

> *"What are the ways I'll be recognized for my gift?"*

With respect to that last question, I have been involved in philanthropy for over 40 years and have met very few anonymous donors! Most people like to have their names associated with worthy, highly-regarded non-profit organizations. As many may be reluctant to ask outright about donor recognition, it is important to address this question proactively.

Before you can engage in meaningful conversations about your organization, it is imperative that you and your colleagues formulate answers to those four crucial questions. While every prospective donor will not necessarily verbalize all of these questions, I can assure you that they will have them in mind. Having answers to these questions will produce a consistent and persuasive message for all of your organization's fundraising efforts.

\* \* \*

*Can you and your organization answer
the four key questions?*

# Donor-Centric Fundraising

Many non-profit organizations have a fundamental flaw in their fundraising perspective: rather than consider what the donors might want – the answers to the "four critical questions" posed in the previous chapter – they present fundraising needs only from their organization's perspective. What *they* need in order to accomplish *their* mission. Funds to finance *their* programs and *their* operating budget. While it is human nature to focus on our own self-interests, that approach in fundraising is a recipe for failure.

The most successful fundraising always focuses on the donor, not on the organization. What **the donor** hopes to accomplish through his or her gift. Funds to finance programs **the donor** has compelling reasons to support. By making this fundamental shift in perspective, organizations begin to regard the donor as central to their institutional thinking for fundraising, which is the recipe for fundraising success.

With that in mind, organizations should incorporate the following donor-centric philosophy into their day-to-day thinking about fundraising: *"The formulation of our fundraising strategies, programs and activities is continually guided by consideration of the donor."*

That donor-centric commitment can lead to:

o **Community/Cause Investment:** Articulating a financial need as a donor investment in the community or a cause, rather than as an organizational prerogative.

o **Donor Acknowledgement:** Ensuring the donor is appropriately and continually acknowledged and recognized for gift support at all levels and intentions.

o **Donor Stewardship:** Encourage the donor's ongoing involvement and support with evidence that both prior as well as future gifts have great impact.

\* \* \*

*Is your organization more focused on its needs rather than donors' need to know they are making a valued investment in aiding people through your programs and services?*

# Why People Give

There have been many studies conducted over the years to determine what motivates people to make charitable contributions. A list of the top reasons that inspire donors to give follows. Rather than guessing what might encourage potential donors to support your organization, you should incorporate as many motivating factors as possible into your organization's printed materials, public announcements, podium presentations and, most importantly, meaningful conversations with potential supporters.

**Community Responsibility**..."giving back" to where they live or conduct business

**Competitiveness**...matching competitors or maintain a perceived social position

**Merit**...because the organization deserves it

**Quid Pro Quo**...to return for, or to encourage a favor

**Altruism**...pure philanthropy!

**Religious Principles**...fulfilling a stated or unstated religious commitment

**Recognition**...public acknowledgement of their support

**Personal Satisfaction**...because it makes them feel good

**Tax Deduction**...because Uncle Sam picks up some of the cost

**Pressure**...from peers, customers, employees or employers

**Social Custom**...galas, theatre benefits, charity auctions

**Intimate Understanding**...because they've "been there"

**Habit**...as with alumni or church giving

**Edifice Urge**...the "monument builders"

**Sympathy**...for those less fortunate, e.g. homeless people, injured veterans

**Self–Protection**...to prevent social unrest or economic burden

**Love**...for a person, principle or institution

**Ambition**...moving up the rungs of the donor honor roll

*Passing and Collecting Chits*..."today it's me, next time it's you!"

*Acquiring Respectability*...securing or regaining a "good person" image

*Debt*...an assumed obligation

\* \* \*

*How many of these motivating factors*
*can you incorporate into your fundraising?*

# Reasons for Not Giving

Sometimes it can seem that volunteers and donors have many more reasons for not joining in fundraising efforts than they have for actively participating.

### Seasonal Reasons

o *Around Thanksgiving, people focus their attention on their families.*

o *Then during Christmas holidays, everyone is gifting and entertaining family and friends.*

o *Then early in the New Year, people are paying off their Christmas bills.*

o *Then spring brings the dreaded tax time of the year.*

o *Then during the summer, people are traveling and generally out-of-touch.*

o   *Then in the fall, families are preparing their children for the new school year.*

o   *And then it's Thanksgiving again!*

### Financial Market Reasons

o   *The stock market is too high...is in a downward trend...is uncertain.*

o   *Interest rates are too high...may go lower...are erratic.*

o   *The global economy is overheated...is disintegrating...is unpredictable.*

### Personal Reasons

o   *"I give to other charitable organizations."*

o   *"My spouse isn't interested."*

o   *"I'm too busy to consider any other involvement."*

o   *"Your organization should focus on foundations and corporations where the real money is."*

When you find yourself getting discouraged by statements like these from donors and volunteers, engage them in a Socratic exercise: ask related questions to gain a better understanding of their objections. Their responses may lead them to changing their own minds! For example:

*"When would be a better time to discuss this? Hoping, of course, that you are interested in helping the people we serve."*

*"May I contact you again when the stock market reaches more optimistic levels? When interest rates adjust significantly? When you feel our nation's economy is headed in a better direction?"*

*"I would never ask you to put our organization ahead of other worthy causes you support. But could we move up your list a bit?"*

*"Perhaps if we met with you and your spouse together?"*

*"What could we do that might encourage you to reconsider your involvement and support?"*

*"We would appreciate your suggestions regarding foundations and corporation that support us. Can you be helpful in contacting them?"*

A final thought: polite persistence pays!

\* \* \*

**_Is your organization politely persistent in seeking and securing support?_**

# Cultivating Your Major Donors

When funding needs are pressing, your instinct to quickly secure a major gift is no substitute for thoughtful cultivation of major donors' interests. You should assume that your potential major donors are seasoned and sensible stewards of their financial resources. As such, they will:

o   Want to be assured that the plans they are being asked to fund result from thoughtful and sound planning and not the sudden inspiration of your organization eager to get their money.

o   Want to know that others support the organization, especially the governing Board, and that they have not been singled out for a gift just because they have significant financial means.

o   Want to be persuaded that the funding need is an urgent one, essential to be met now and not at some future indefinite time.

In my experience, some recurring themes tend to feature prominently in an individual's eventual decision to make a major gift:

o   Major donors tend to relate to **institutional vision** and **leadership**: a vision of what can be achieved well beyond current fundraising goals, promoted by leadership that inspires confidence in achieving that vision.

o   Major donors want to know that their gifts **make a difference** in meeting a compelling need, and are not to shore-up the need for sound fiscal management.

o   Major gifts reflect the donor's level of **involvement** with the organization, an involvement courted not simply for their capacity to give but for a more intimate role in the organization's governance, programs and services.

* * *

*Does your organization offer potential major donors a vision and leadership to inspire their support?*

# Preparing Yourself
# To Secure Major Gifts

Volunteers and professionals alike, old hands or new comers to fundraising, should prepare themselves prior to making personal contact with potential major donors.

### An Overview

*Be comfortable.* Each person has a comfortable personal style for persuasion. There are no hard and fast rules for securing major gifts commitments. Be comfortable. Be candid. Admit what you may not know, but can certainly find out. You can't make a mistake in wanting to help others benefit from your organization's services and programs.

*You are not asking for yourself*. You are offering an opportunity for a caring individual to provide for others who may be less fortunate.

*You can't fail*. Fundraising experiences have shown that 50% to 65% of people personally contacted and met with will eventually make a contribution. The great value of you personally *"telling the story"* is that 100% of the people you engage with will know much more about your organization than before you talked with them. So you can't fail!

***Persistence and patience pays***. Fundraising experiences have also shown that it can take 6 to 18 months of multiple conversations and meetings to secure an individual's major gift commitment. Polite persistence and thoughtful follow-up will demonstrate to potential major donors the importance of your efforts. "One-shot" attempts much less so!

***Mini-Campaigns.*** Consider each potential major donor a "mini-campaign" requiring a thoughtful approach and understanding of the individual's interests, circumstances, and relationships. Much of which can be learned from careful listening during your personal contacts.

### Anticipating Questions

Anticipating thoughtful questions a potential major donor might ask, or would certainly have on his/her mind, is the best preparation for your personal contact. As well as helping you gain confidence in your approach. If you don't have answers to any of the following questions, or others you may have, ask the staff at your organization to suggest responses.

> *"Has the Board made their contributions to the effort? If so, what is the percentage and aggregate dollar amount?"*

*"What happens if you don't reach the expressed dollar goal in a timely manner?"*

*"Is the organization prepared to finance a portion of the projected costs; for example for 'bridge' or 'gap' financing in order to move forward with the project in a timely manner in the event contributions fall short?"*

*"Who is leading the fundraising effort as volunteers?"*

*"Who is providing professional support for the fundraising effort?"*

*"What are the anticipated fundraising-related costs, and is that amount included in the fundraising dollar goal?"*

*"How confident are you that the dollar goal is sufficient, when reached, to fund both direct and indirect costs of the project?"*

*"What are the anticipated added costs to the organization's overall operating budget when the new facilities are built and new programs operational? And, how will those added costs be funded, i.e. endowment income, government contracts and grants, increased annual giving?"*

*"How long will I have to make payments on my pledge: 2 to 3 years; 5 years; 10 years?"*

*"How long do you expect this fundraising effort to run?"*

*"Will there be donor recognition opportunities, and how will my family be recognized?"*

\* \* \*

**Are you adequately prepared for your major gift prospect contacts?**

# Major Donors:
# Interest - Inform - Involve

Americans are inundated daily with television, radio, internet, text and print media messages urging them to purchase, vote, support, and undertake countless other actions and activities. With over 1.4 million non-profit organizations throughout the United States competing for peoples' time, attention and resources the competition for major donors is intense.

Consequently, when seeking potential major donors the applied strategy should be to first gain their interest... before attempting in inform them in detail about your organization ...before attempting to involve them in any meaningful ways through their charitable donations and volunteer efforts. That process could take one meeting or several, over one week or one year. But lurching ahead too swiftly may lose their interest and subsequently their involvement.

## Fast Facts

One of the best ways to capture someone's initial interest is to offer some 'fast facts' intended to capture their attention, and encourage them to become more informed about your organization. Facts that can lead to such responses as: *"Oh, I didn't know they did that...for that many people....with those results!"*

## From the Donor's Perspective

The most successful fundraising always focuses on the donor, not on the organization. What the donor hopes to accomplish through his or her gift, not how much the organization needs to raise. By making this fundamental shift in perspective, organizations begin to regard the donor as central to their institutional thinking and planning for fundraising.

\* \* \*

### *Do you have your 'Fast Facts'?*

# Today's Major Donors
# and Top Volunteers

Those of us involved in philanthropy professionally need to be mindful of people we depend on to support the organizations we serve. And, we have to consider their points-of-view if we are to engage them in meaningful ways to the benefit our organizations.

Following are some perspectives to consider in working with your organization's leadership.

**Many of Today's Major Donors...**

o   New wealth... mainly through entrepreneurial activities

o   Want things to be done quickly

o   See their money as a tool, and not a commodity

o   Think "outside the box"

o   Competitive and driven to excel

- o  Few philanthropic role models

- o  "High finance" is their frame of reference

- o  "Hands-on investors" rather than passive donors

- o  Evaluate decisions from a sound business plan

- o  Limited tolerance for long or complex presentations

**Many of Today's Top Volunteers...**

- o  Strong-willed and inexperienced in campaigning

- o  Urge "big asks" on an aggressive timetable

- o  "Case" and funding needs must be based on hard facts and statistics

- o  Few meetings... limited hierarchical structuring... impatient with "training"

- o  Limited tolerance for frequent and lengthy meetings

- o  "Business metrics" approach to evaluate performance and results

\* \* \*

*How are you being mindful of the points-of-view of your major donors and top volunteers?*

# Prospect Profiling

Organizations which are developing their fundraising programs often want a sample. Format and content to use in gathering public and available background information on their major donors. The following pages illustrate an example.

**Prospect Profiling**

Date Latest Information Entered: _____By: _____

| Contact Information |
| :---: |

Check box for preferred contact information:

Full Name:_____

☐ Home Address:_____zip:_____
☐ Home Phone:_____
☐ Personal Email: _____
Company/Firm Name:

_____

☐ Business Address:_____zip:_____

☐ Business Title: _____

☐ Business Phone: _____

☐ Business Email _____

Spouse's Name: _____

Children Names/Ages: _____

## Financial/Volunteer Information

### Contributions

Annual: $ _____

Capital: $ _____

Special Events: $_____

### Volunteer Involvement

Our Organization: _____

Other Organizations: _____

### Wealth Screening

Liquid Assets: $_____

Fixed Assets: $_____

Philanthropic Giving: $_____

Property $_____

Securities: $_____

## Prospect Management/Stewardship

### Date:    Action Item:

_____/_____

_____/_____

_____/_____

_____/_____

_____/_____

_____/_____

_____/_____

## Comments

# Donor Recognition

Establishing donor recognition policies and procedures should be tailored to an organization's prior experiences and sensibilities. With that in mind, the following are suggested general policies and procedures to consider.

### Donor Recognition Objectives

The overall objectives of thoughtful donor recognition plan are to:

o   Honor donors at established dollar levels for acknowledgement on a published or permanent "honor roll" as well as "naming" major features and facilities.

o   Encourage donors to continue their support and involvement with the organization.

### Donor Recognition Committee

A Donor Recognition Committee can be appointed comprised of several Board members and senior staff to guide and direct the organization's formal recognition of donors. This Committee's principal areas of responsibility would be to:

o   Review current policies and procedures related to donor recognition, and make any suggested additions and/or modifications judged necessary.

o   Oversee the application of approved donor recognition policies, as well as make any necessary *exceptions to policy* as judged to be in the best interests of the organization and donors involved.

o   Oversee the preparation and placement of donor plaques and honor rolls as well as receptions, mementoes and the like designed to honor donors.

### Number and Levels of Naming Opportunities

A sufficient number of naming opportunities should be identified at the appropriate gift dollar levels to coincide with a projected gift model for a capital campaign.

### Right of First Acceptance

During initial personal contacts and conversations with potential major donors, and prior to formal Board approval of donor naming recognition policies and procedures, early donors/donor families can be assured of their "right of first acceptance" of Board approved naming opportunities based on the date and level of their gift commitment.

## Gift Policies for Naming

The following general guidelines would be applied to terms and conditions for naming a major facility or feature:

o **Cash-In-Hand:** The formal and official naming of a major facility or feature will be made when a specified percent, e.g. 50% of the confirmed pledge has been received from the donor/donor family toward their total pledged commitment.

o **Pledge Periods:** Gifts pledged with payments of up to a specified number of years will be acceptable for naming.

o **Will Codicils**: Donors at the highest gift levels, e.g. $ 1 million and above would be asked to consider a codicil to their will/estate plans incorporating the terms and conditions of their gift commitment.

## Expectations of Timing for Naming

In accepting naming gifts, the organization must be clear with donors, and donors must be willing to accept reasonable expectations of timing and/or other specific considerations under which the major facility or feature will be constructed or renovated.

Donors of estate planned gifts should be listed separately and distinctly from donors of cash and cash equivalent gifts. An estate planned gift with a face value of $100,000 is not the same magnitude of worth as a $100,000 cash commitment.

> **Note:** While there are other policies and procedures that would govern specific organizations' donor recognition policies and procedures, such stipulations should be reviewed by an organization's legal counsel and financial advisor to ensure the resulting gift meets both the donor's wishes and the organization's funding needs.

* * *

**Does your organization have in place adequate donor recognition policies and procedures?**

# Communicating with Your Constituencies

*"No one knows what we do!" "We're the best kept secret in town!"*
*"Our light is under a bushel basket!" "Why isn't anyone 'getting'*
*our message?"*

When I hear laments like these from non-profit organizations, it tells me that they are probably not communicating as effectively as they could with key constituencies. It's a common problem that can very often be addressed by applying some tried-and-true communication principles.

## Keep Your Messages Clear and Consistent

People can't get your message if you don't really have one. Know clearly what you do, what you need and what your organization stands for – that's your first step. Then you have to be able to articulate those messages plainly and succinctly, with commonly understood words rather than with references and terms unique to your organization. Remember, too, that your messages should capture attention and not overwhelm the reader/listener with too much information. Finally, make sure that all of the

THE ART OF FUNDRAISING

"communicators" in your organization know your core message –
sometimes referred to as the "elevator speech" – and how to share
it in a clear and consistent manner.

## Repetition is Essential

An axiom in the advertising profession is that by the time account
executives are bored with a client's advertising message, the public
is just starting to catch on. While you and your Board have heard
your organization's message over and over again, don't assume
that others will "get it" from scanning your newsletter, annual
report or solicitation materials. Repetition of your fundamental
mission, notable accomplishments and distinguishing goals is
essential to communicate your organization's merit and clearly,
precisely and continually create the strongest possible case for
charitable support.

## The Ripple Effect from Personal Messaging

Public relations studies show that the average individual
interacts with 200 to 300 people a year; the more prominent
and influential the individual, the more personal interactions
he or she is likely to have. When you or your Board members
engage influencers in meaningful conversation about your
organization that person will likely repeat that same strong

message to others. With this exponential impact you can't fail to boost support!

* * *

*How well is your organization communicating with key constituencies?*

# Make Your Messages Work

Some things to remember when you formulate messages to persuade people to support your organization:

## Major Donors Fund the Future, not the Past

While statements of your accomplishments and evidence of your financial stability are important, it's the future – not the past – that most interests major donors. Make sure you articulate a clear and engaging vision for the future.

## Major Donors Are Interested in Helping People

Improving the lives of others is what most inspires major donors; they may care less about the programs designed to deliver those results. Focus on what a donor's gift will mean to the people your organization assists rather than how the gift will shape your organization.

## Talk "Loud and Proud"

The most effective communicators are often volunteers who talk "loud and proud" about your organization, rather than professional staff who are seen as paid to persuade. Educate your Board members and volunteers about your organization's strengths and impact and encourage them to go out and spread the word. For Board members who may be reticent to speak out, I suggest some one-on-one sessions with a self-confident and persuasive Board member.

## Change Requires Patience and Persistence

Changing people's perspectives about your organization, especially if they start out as uninformed, ambivalent, or even negative, takes patience and persistence. As it is hard to predict the exact time and place when your message will be "heard" by your prospective donor, polite persistence will catch the prospective donor when they are most receptive.

\* \* \*

**Do your messages work for your organization?**

# Encouraging Unrestricted Contributions

All non-profit organizations recognize the value of unrestricted contributions. These gifts are given without donor designated end-use and are to be used for any purpose by the organization, most of which use it for general operating purposes. Despite being well aware of their value, many non-profit organizations fail to persuade donors to give unrestricted contributions.

It is important to remember that donors most often are motivated to give based on their understanding of how their contribution will likely impact the lives of others. With an understanding of that motivation, an effective way to encourage unrestricted contributions is to "bundle" selected annual operating costs associated with prominent programs or activities, and represent those programs or activities for sponsorship in the name of donors.

For example, the annual cost of an after-school program is $25,000, including allocated staff compensation, materials and supplies, transportation, participant financial assistance. You may be able to encourage a donor to support that program as a sponsor, or, alternatively, endow the program in perpetuity. In that way the organization's previously budgeted funds for that program can be reallocated to other pressing funding needs, or for the organization's long-term "financial sustainability" through allocation to permanent endowment.

This approach is similar to "naming" a major feature within a new building for a donor. This does not signify that the donor's contribution was used to fund that specific "named" room, gallery, or auditorium. It merely signifies that the organization is able to honor the donor's generosity through such "naming". So it is with sponsored programs and activities: providing meaningful recognition by associating the donors' name with a specific program or activity.

In this manner the donor is acknowledged for sponsorship of a specific program, and the organization can reallocate previously budgeted funds to meet other pressing financial needs. A real "win-win" for the donor and the organization!

* * *

**How is your organization encouraging unrestricted contributions?**

# THE PEOPLE

Volunteer and staff leadership is an essential "front and center" force in our nation's non-profit sector. This leadership takes many forms. Leadership to oversee stewardship of funds received, granted and expended. Leadership to bring heightened public prominence of their organizations' valued services. Leadership to ensure that sound professional management is guiding the organization's programs and policies.

# There's No Getting Around Leadership

When it comes to successful fundraising, there's no getting around the need for dedicated, engaged Board leadership. Your organization may have a solid "case" to attract gift support, an ample number of potential major donors and a constituency that recognizes its vital mission – all of which are important. But without Board leadership in securing major gift support, it's not likely that your organization will be able to financially sustain its most valued goals and objectives.

## A Board Member's Fundraising Leadership Checklist

Here's a checklist for your Board members to use to measure their fundraising leadership, and to judge how many fundraising-related functions they are both willing and able to perform.

o   I have a clear understanding of the organization's mission, goals and funding priorities.

o  I understand and fully endorse the "case" for donor support of the organization.

o  I contribute to the fullest measure within my financial means.

o  I assist staff in identifying and evaluating potential major donors.

o  I share in the personal contact and "cultivation" of potential major donors.

o  I make introductions for others to make gift solicitation visits.

o  I am willing to accompany others on gift solicitation visits.

o  I write personal follow-up and gift acknowledgement letters.

o  I take every opportunity to compliment professional staff for their fundraising work and accomplishments.

o  If necessary, I am prepared to directly solicit a gift from a potential major donor.

o  I do what I say I will do.

* * *

**What are your Board members doing in fundraising?**

# Secrets to a More Effective Board

Do these laments sound familiar? *"Our Board members check their brains at the door before a meeting."* Or, *"They don't give us much of their time or expertise."* Or, *"It's just not a fundraising Board!"* I've heard versions of these common complaints over and over again. Yet when I investigate, I often find that the Board members in question are willing and even eager to become more engaged in fundraising and other meaningful activities to support their chosen non-profit organizations.

So where is the disconnect?

The vast majority of Board members are talented, dedicated men and women. They are true community leaders, keenly interested in promoting the success of their organization's mission. However – and this is the unspoken but glaringly obvious truth – they seldom volunteer! They tend to remain "standing ready" until specifically and individually asked to take on meaningful tasks and assignments. If there's a secret formula for optimizing the participation and value of your Board, it's this: ASK!

As with potential major donors, Board members need to be asked – personally, precisely and persuasively. Some suggestions to assist you in encouraging your Board members to become more engaged:

o Articulate clearly and in writing the Board's roles and responsibilities, with meaningful goals and expectations. Periodically report on progress made toward meeting those objectives.

o Meet at least once a year with each Board member to determine what he/she is most able and willing to accomplish on behalf of the organization. Confirm those "understandings" in writing with periodic follow-up to encourage the Board member's efforts.

o View and solicit Board members as potential donors. Don't presume that they will be generous just because they are "on the Board." As with any potential major donor, they need to be persuaded by a compelling case, urgent funding priorities, appropriate donor recognition, and a personal "ask".

o Provide for annual self-evaluations by Board members, as well as evaluations of the Board as a whole.

\* \* \*

*Are you doing everything you can to engage your Board members?*

# Taking Board Recruitment Seriously

Most non-profit organizations aspire to a high caliber of Board leadership. However, many organizations select their Board members in what can only be described as an arbitrary and casual manner. Too often, the Board recruitment process neglects to pose the kind of thoughtful questions that a candidate with stature in his/her profession and community would expect when being considered for an important position.

The following are some questions that can be used to identify and evaluate serious candidates for your Board.

o   What is your general impression of our organization based on comments you have heard or read over the past several years?

o   In your experience, what have you observed to be the most essential role of a Board member serving a non-profit organization?

o   In your view, what are some of the most important tasks a Board member can be asked to undertake on behalf of his/her organization?

o  Which of the non-profit organizations you have worked with make the most effective use of their Board leadership? In what ways?

o  Do you have any constraints on your time or availability that might influence your active participation as a Board member?

o  Are there any specific tasks or operational areas that you would prefer not to be actively engaged with as a Board member?

o  With respect to your charitable contributions, where would you most likely direct your support for our organization?

o  Is there additional information you would need before asking others to support our organization in significant ways?

The responses are often remarkably illuminating!

\* \* \*

**How would your current Board members respond to these questions?**

# Value of a Board Audit

It's a common scenario. Board members have the feeling that things are "just not going right" with their organization, but they lack either sufficient information or the necessary courage to raise sensitive issues. Consequently, a non-profit organization can go on for years operating under a cloud of uneasiness or with an absence of meaningful involvement from the governing Board.

Under these circumstances, when a Board audit is finally called for, there is a perception of deep dissatisfaction which raises considerable anxiety within the organization. However, when periodic Board audits are built into the framework of your organization, conducted in a scheduled and non–threatening manner, much good can result. The Board stays informed and involved; issues that might otherwise be neglected are acknowledged and addressed in a timely way; and there is a defined, consistent process in place for healthy organizational review.

Here's how it can be done:

Bylaw Article *Example*: **BOARD AUDIT AND REVIEW COMMITTEE.** There shall be an audit and review of each of the following aspects of the organization, with each aspect examined at least once every five (5) years, with one aspect examined in depth each year.

1.  The organization's services and programs

2.  The organization's business and physical plant management

3.  The organization's fundraising and financing

4.  Activities and performance of the Chief Executive and senior staff

These audits and reviews shall be conducted by a Committee appointed by the Board Chairman, and shall report results to the full Board. The Chairperson of this Committee shall be a member of the governing Board.

\* \* \*

***Can your organization benefit from periodic,
non–threatening Board audits?***

# Board Profile

When considering the qualifications of potential Board members, it's essential to examine the profile of your Board as a whole. What skills, expertise, abilities and know-how do your current Board members bring to your organization? What qualities are missing from your current Board that you should actively look for in new members?

To answer those important questions, I've found the following *Board Profile* particularly helpful. By inventorying the specific skills and expertise of current Board members, it can make clear at a glance which talents and abilities you most need from new members.

# BOARD PROFILE - Expertise and Skills

| Area of Expertise/Skills | Current Board Members | | | | | | | | | | | | | | | New Board Candidates | | | |
|---|---|---|---|---|---|---|---|---|---|---|---|---|---|---|---|---|---|---|---|
| | 1 | 2 | 3 | 4 | 5 | 6 | 7 | 8 | 9 | 10 | 11 | 12 | 13 | 14 | 15 | A | B | C | D |
| Administrator | | | | | | | | | | | | | | | | | | | |
| Business/Corporate | | | | | | | | | | | | | | | | | | | |
| Community Leader | | | | | | | | | | | | | | | | | | | |
| Educator | | | | | | | | | | | | | | | | | | | |
| Executive Director | | | | | | | | | | | | | | | | | | | |
| Finance: | | | | | | | | | | | | | | | | | | | |
| Accounting | | | | | | | | | | | | | | | | | | | |
| Banking & Trust | | | | | | | | | | | | | | | | | | | |
| Investments | | | | | | | | | | | | | | | | | | | |
| Foundation Representative | | | | | | | | | | | | | | | | | | | |
| Fundraising | | | | | | | | | | | | | | | | | | | |
| Government Representative | | | | | | | | | | | | | | | | | | | |
| Health Care | | | | | | | | | | | | | | | | | | | |
| Human Resources | | | | | | | | | | | | | | | | | | | |
| Insurance | | | | | | | | | | | | | | | | | | | |
| Legal | | | | | | | | | | | | | | | | | | | |
| Marketing | | | | | | | | | | | | | | | | | | | |
| Media | | | | | | | | | | | | | | | | | | | |
| Entertainment | | | | | | | | | | | | | | | | | | | |
| Public Relations | | | | | | | | | | | | | | | | | | | |
| Real Estate | | | | | | | | | | | | | | | | | | | |
| Recruiting | | | | | | | | | | | | | | | | | | | |
| Strategic Planning | | | | | | | | | | | | | | | | | | | |
| Administrator | | | | | | | | | | | | | | | | | | | |
| Special Program Focus | | | | | | | | | | | | | | | | | | | |
| Board Committees: | | | | | | | | | | | | | | | | | | | |
| President | | | | | | | | | | | | | | | | | | | |
| Officer | | | | | | | | | | | | | | | | | | | |
| Development | | | | | | | | | | | | | | | | | | | |
| Finance | | | | | | | | | | | | | | | | | | | |
| Marketing | | | | | | | | | | | | | | | | | | | |
| Nominating | | | | | | | | | | | | | | | | | | | |
| Planning | | | | | | | | | | | | | | | | | | | |

# BOARD PROFILE
## Additional Considerations

| Area of Expertise/Skills | Current Board Members | | | | | | | | | | | | | | | New Board Candidates | | | |
|---|---|---|---|---|---|---|---|---|---|---|---|---|---|---|---|---|---|---|---|
| | 1 | 2 | 3 | 4 | 5 | 6 | 7 | 8 | 9 | 10 | 11 | 12 | 13 | 14 | 15 | A | B | C | D |
| **Age:** | | | | | | | | | | | | | | | | | | | |
| Under 35 | | | | | | | | | | | | | | | | | | | |
| From 36 to 50 | | | | | | | | | | | | | | | | | | | |
| From 51 to 65 | | | | | | | | | | | | | | | | | | | |
| Over 65 | | | | | | | | | | | | | | | | | | | |
| **Gender:** | | | | | | | | | | | | | | | | | | | |
| Women | | | | | | | | | | | | | | | | | | | |
| Men | | | | | | | | | | | | | | | | | | | |
| **Race/Ethnic Background:** | | | | | | | | | | | | | | | | | | | |
| African-American | | | | | | | | | | | | | | | | | | | |
| Asian | | | | | | | | | | | | | | | | | | | |
| Hispanic/Latino | | | | | | | | | | | | | | | | | | | |
| Native American | | | | | | | | | | | | | | | | | | | |
| Caucasian | | | | | | | | | | | | | | | | | | | |
| Other | | | | | | | | | | | | | | | | | | | |
| **Geographic Location:** | | | | | | | | | | | | | | | | | | | |
| City | | | | | | | | | | | | | | | | | | | |
| Suburbs | | | | | | | | | | | | | | | | | | | |
| State | | | | | | | | | | | | | | | | | | | |
| County | | | | | | | | | | | | | | | | | | | |
| **Contribution:** In-Kind (I), Donation (D) | | | | | | | | | | | | | | | | | | | |
| > 10K | | | | | | | | | | | | | | | | | | | |
| 5-10K | | | | | | | | | | | | | | | | | | | |
| 2-5K | | | | | | | | | | | | | | | | | | | |
| 1-2K | | | | | | | | | | | | | | | | | | | |
| <1K | | | | | | | | | | | | | | | | | | | |
| **Length of Board Service:** | | | | | | | | | | | | | | | | | | | |
| Over 10 Years | | | | | | | | | | | | | | | | | | | |
| 5 to 10 Years | | | | | | | | | | | | | | | | | | | |
| 2 to 4 Years | | | | | | | | | | | | | | | | | | | |
| Less than 2 Years | | | | | | | | | | | | | | | | | | | |
| **Meeting Attendance:** | | | | | | | | | | | | | | | | | | | |
| 75 - 100% | | | | | | | | | | | | | | | | | | | |
| 50 - 74% | | | | | | | | | | | | | | | | | | | |
| 20 - 49% | | | | | | | | | | | | | | | | | | | |
| < 20% | | | | | | | | | | | | | | | | | | | |

\* \* \*

*Do you know what your Board Profile looks like?*

# Board Self-Evaluation Checklist

I have found that in developing Board leadership it is useful to periodically ask Board members to individually evaluate the Board as a whole from their unique perspectives and experiences. Individual responses can and should be kept confidential; the value of this exercise comes from the resulting composite of member evaluations. Periodic Board self-evaluation often leads to important insights about the Board's role in your organization, and both positive and negative responses provide useful direction for "next steps" in Board development.

# BOARD SELF-EVALUATION QUESTIONNAIRE

## Board Role

| Yes | No | Uncertain | |
|:---:|:---:|:---:|---|
| ❏ | ❏ | ❏ | Board members are familiar with our organization's history, and understand its mission to serve our community. |
| ❏ | ❏ | ❏ | Our Board members understand their primary role is as policy-makers, and delegate day-to-day management of this non-profit organization to the administrator. |
| ❏ | ❏ | ❏ | The Board recognizes its responsibility to employ an administrator, and to reconfirm confidence in him/her each year by conducting a performance evaluation. |
| ❏ | ❏ | ❏ | Board members are active advocates who promote the interests of our organization and the people we serve, i.e. they talk "loud and proud" about our work. |
| ❏ | ❏ | ❏ | Our Board members offer their personal expertise and advice understanding that in this role they act as outside consultants whose services and counsel may be accepted, rejected or modified by the administrator. |

## Board Responsibilities and Policies

| Yes | No | Uncertain | |
|:---:|:---:|:---:|---|
| ❏ | ❏ | ❏ | Our Board has an established a committee structure which provides oversight of our organization's finances, operations, fundraising, facilities and programs in addition to selecting new Board members. |
| ❏ | ❏ | ❏ | We have a policy that requires Board members to channel all questions, responses or complaints from the public or news media to our administrator. |
| ❏ | ❏ | ❏ | We periodically review all Board policies and procedures to ensure they are in compliance with federal, state and local regulations as well as responsive to the present-day requirements of our organization. |
| ❏ | ❏ | ❏ | Our Board members are indemnified by Directors and Officers Insurance, and know the extent and limitations of this coverage. |

## Board Fundraising

| Yes | No | Uncertain | |
|-----|-----|-----------|---|
| ❑ | ❑ | ❑ | Each Board member is expected to make an annual unrestricted contribution, each to his/her own level of financial means, in addition to an occasional "over and above" gift commitment in support of a Board approved major fundraising campaign. |
| ❑ | ❑ | ❑ | We expect all Board members to be actively involved in ways they can be most helpful in the organization's fundraising activities and events. |

## Board Membership

| Yes | No | Uncertain | |
|-----|-----|-----------|---|
| ❑ | ❑ | ❑ | Board members recognize their responsibility to identify and encourage, through an established nominating process, qualified candidates to fill Board vacancies. |
| ❑ | ❑ | ❑ | All new Board members receive a formal orientation focusing on the elements of this *Board Self-Evaluation Checklist*. |
| ❑ | ❑ | ❑ | We have clearly-articulated position descriptions for Board members as well as task descriptions for each Board committee. |
| ❑ | ❑ | ❑ | Our formal Board meetings are conducted in a manner which encourages Board member participation, and do not unreasonably extend the time to conduct Board business. |
| ❑ | ❑ | ❑ | The Board formally evaluates its own performance annually. |

## Board Strategic Planning

| Yes | No | Uncertain | |
|-----|-----|-----------|---|
| ❑ | ❑ | ❑ | The Board recognizes the importance of strategic planning, and has established near- and long-term goals with reasonable and measurable objectives to be met. |
| ❑ | ❑ | ❑ | Board members review, evaluate and update as necessary our organization's strategic plan at least once a year. |

\* \* \*

## *Does your Board understand its role in your organization?*

# Role of the Fundraising Professional

There's no question that the success of an organization's fundraising is dependent, in large measure, on capable and dedicated professional staff. However, it's important that development professionals recognize that their distinctive role is based on a fundamental fundraising equation:

## *The "90/10" Equation*

o   Fundraising professionals should be expected to do 90 percent of the work and receive 10 percent of the credit for fundraising success.

o   Fundraising volunteers should receive 90 percent of the credit for accomplishing 10 percent of the work, i.e. securing financial and leadership commitments.

# The "90/10" Checklist
## for the Fundraising Professional

❑ Do you consistently apply the *"90/10" Equation* in working with your volunteers?

❑ Are you patient with volunteers, recognizing that they have personal and professional time priorities ahead of their volunteer fundraising commitments?

❑ Do you offer prompt and valued assistance to volunteers to help them meet their acknowledged fundraising goals?

❑ Do you take advantage of the diverse talents and varied availability of volunteers?

❑ Do you keep volunteers well–informed but not over–burdened with information and paperwork?

❑ Do you listen carefully to volunteer ideas and suggestions and candidly assess their practicality based on the organization's policies and goals?

❑ Do you actively assist volunteers in the cultivation and solicitation of potential major donors?

❑ Do you do what you say you will do in a timely manner?

\* \* \*

*How do the fundraising professionals*
*in your organization check out?*

# Querying a Candidate

Attempting to hire a skilled and experienced Development Officer is an exercise in frustration for many non-profit organizations. That's because, despite the importance of this decision, the recruitment process often involves a rather shallow questioning of candidates. When vetting candidates for the crucial role of Development Officer, non-profit leadership should ask the following probing questions – and then listen with great care and attention to ascertain how the answers mesh with the goals and culture of their organization:

o   What do you consider to be your single most noteworthy accomplishment in your current/previous position?

o   What do you think is the most important quality necessary for success in fundraising?

o   How do you handle being under the gun? How do you get others to help in those situations?

o   What kinds of failures have you experienced, and what have you learned from those experiences?

o   What will we hear when we speak with the people you've listed as references? What will they say about you?

o   What are some of your fundraising prejudices?

o   How would you describe your leadership style?

o   What are you most enthusiastic about?

o   How do you resolve professional conflicts?

* * *

**How would you respond to these questions?**

# 8 Tips in Hiring Development Officers

With the reported rapid turnover in Development Officers throughout the non-profit sector, the following tips taken from **The NonProfit Times** can be helpful.

1. **Let Them Speak:** Some involved in hiring make the mistake of talking too much about themselves, leaving little time for the candidate to talk. While it is important to let the candidate know as much as possible about the organization and the position, you also need to know as much as possible about the candidate so you can make the most informed employment decision.

2. **Involve Other Staff Members:** Having others interview the candidate will inform him/her about your non-profit's culture. Even more useful for your purposes, it will also give you multiple perspectives on the candidate.

3. **Prepare Questions:** Prepare a list of questions that you absolutely must have the answers to know if the

individual will be a "good fit" at the organization.

4. **Impress:** Remember that the interview is not just about whether you like the candidate; it's also about whether the candidate likes you and the organization.

5. **Offer a Competitive Salary:** If you encounter a truly worthy candidate, don't be afraid to offer a salary that is a little higher than market indicates. Money does talk, after all.

6. **Do Your Homework:** Do a little digging into the candidate's past to see how they performed at previous employers.

7. **Pay Attention to Details:** Sometimes the small things can be the biggest indicator of how a candidate will perform. Was the candidate dressed appropriately? How was his/her body language? These are all things you need to observe.

8. **Trust Your Instincts:** If your instinct tells you an applicant is too good to be true, you should probably heed it. Don't proceed with hiring until your concerns are alleviated.

\* \* \*

*Have you been effective in hiring people who work well in your organization?*

# Commission Based Fundraising

Occasionally I am asked if a fundraising professional should be compensated on the basis of a percentage of funds he/she raises. The presented rationale typically is *"that's the way we do it in business... basing compensation on production!"* Not unreasonable to consider but definitely not a sound policy in the non-profit sector.

I hasten to point out a distinction between "commission" and "bonus". A commission is a percentage of the financial transaction, or in this case, a gift commitment.  A bonus is a reward for overall performance.

My view regarding commissions is not based solely on ethical standards adopted by professional fundraising associations throughout the United States. My view is also based on practical considerations that commission based compensation can diminish an organization's fundraising results.

> **What Attracts the Gift?**  Donors are primarily attracted to a non-profit organization's fundamental mission, and by a merited regard for its programs, services and reputation

established over years. Not primarily in response to a professional fundraiser's entreaties.

**Who Should Get the Credit?** Most major gifts come after time, patience and personal contacts with a donor by many people associated with the organization, most particularly volunteers. With that in mind, who should receive credit and related bonus for the eventual gift commitment?

**Downgrading Major Gifts:** Donors likely would be reluctant to make a major contribution to a favored organization if they knew that 5% to 10% of their gift went directly to a professional fundraiser involved.

**Premature Solicitations**: A professional fundraiser might be more interested in "closing" a gift commitment swiftly for the immediate compensation, rather than working with the donor over time to maximize his/her interest and eventual gift commitment.

**Unwarranted Promises**: A professional fundraiser might be tempted to suggest special benefits and privileges to encourage a major gift commitment; benefits which the organization may not be in a position to honor. For example: preferential ticketing/seating, discounted medical services or tuition, "naming" a major facility or endowed fund.

**When to Compensate?** How would a professional fundraiser be compensated for a donor's pledge to be paid over five years? In advance before pledge payments are received? As pledge payments are received? When all pledge payments have been received? And, what about an estate planned gift commitment such as bequests and trusts?

**Volunteer Involvement:** It would be difficult to encourage volunteers to become engaged in personal contact, cultivation and solicitation of donors knowing that the assigned fundraiser would be *"taking a cut!"*

\* \* \*

**What are your thoughts about commission based compensation for professional fundraisers?**

# Evaluating Your Development Officer

Increasingly the governing Boards and management of our nation's non-profit institutions have been calling for evaluations of their Development Officers on the basis of their "metrics". They want objective and strictly "by-the-numbers" measurements of the personal contact made with assigned potential donors... leading to the number of donor cultivation events and activities... in turn leading to the number of direct gift solicitations...resulting in indicated dollar gift commitments...all within specified time frames.

While there is nothing inherently wrong with such metric measurements, they fall short of a balanced and comprehensive performance evaluation unless they are combined with assessments of key subjective criteria such as:

o   Boardroom poise, manifested by level of comfort with top executives and community leaders.

o   Ability to work with, motivate, and gain the respect of volunteers.

o Self-initiative to seize opportunities and address concerns that have a direct impact on fundraising.

o Communication skills, both written and oral.

o Ability to establish task priorities and meet agreed-upon deadlines.

o Responsiveness to criticism and advice.

o "Team player" mind-set, demonstrated by the ability to work well with staff members regardless of their hierarchical positions.

\* \* \*

*How do you evaluate your organization's*
*Development Officers?*

# When to Consider Retaining a Consultant

I have recently read a number of articles and advertisements offering advice regarding when to consider retaining a consultant. Most are informative. All are wordy. A few are, perhaps, misleading. In my professional experience there are three basic considerations in determining whether or not to retain a consultant:

o **Experience**: Does the consultant have considerably more experience than you or your colleagues? Is this experience with a number of comparable organizations in area(s) you would like to examine and/or improve?

o **Objectivity**: Would your organization's leadership be more receptive to certain conclusions and recommendations if they were presented by an experienced outside professional who can provide the neutrality and a broader perspective that people closely connected to the organization lack?

o **Time:** Do you and your colleagues not have the necessary time to focus on the area(s) you would like to examine and/or improve? A consultant can focus and not be distracted by the organizational meetings, issues, or upcoming events.

Any one or all of those basic considerations should aid you in determining whether or not to retain a consultant. I also encourage organizations to consider the following:

o   Deciding to retain a consultant requires that the organization has determined it is ready for change.

o   The organization's leadership is ready and willing to work closely with a consultant, and to consider seriously resulting recommendations.

o   At the outset the consultant's assignment goals, working relationships and role are clearly articulated.

o   The organization should provide the consultant with all appropriate background information and understandings of the assignment.

o   While the organization should monitor the consultant's work, don't micromanage the work. Let the consultant do what he or she is being paid for.

* * *

**Are there other requirements you would have in retaining a consultant?**

# Campaign Management
# and Support

Volunteers and professionals not yet experienced in the rigors of planning and conducting a successful major fundraising campaign frequently underestimate the requirements for campaign management and support. All too frequently organizations fail to realize the importance of those requirements until the campaign is well-advanced but well-behind goal expectations.

A number of essential areas of campaign management and support should be addressed early in campaign planning:

o *Key Solicitations: Strategies and Contacts:* Develop individually tailored approaches to identified potential major donors taking into consideration their potential "target" gift level; indicated interest in funding the needs to be addressed; and, persons who could be helpful in encouraging their support. Consider each of these early lead donors, whose combined gift commitments should result in 50 percent to 60 percent of your total campaign fundraising goal, as "mini-campaigns".

o **Campaign Management: Policies and Procedures:**
Determine guidelines for policies such as donor
"naming" recognition; crediting of gift commitments
to designated purposes; timing of construction
commencement based on prudent financial planning;
crediting pledges and estate planning gifts.

o **Campaign Promotion: Public and Donor Relations:**
Design a plan for announcing newsworthy events such
as major gifts and volunteer leadership enlistments,
timed over the course of the campaign to stimulate
campaign fundraising and volunteer involvement.

o **Prospect Research and Communication:** Identify
your donor constituencies, and tailor campaign
communications to personalize messages during
subsequent stages of sequential gift solicitations, i.e.
higher to lower gift levels phased over the course of
the campaign.

o **Campaign Evaluation and Budgeting:** Establish
standards and practices to periodically evaluate the
campaign's progress and cost/effectiveness.

o **Data and Word Processing Systems:** Ensure you
have a data base management system to both retain
gathered information as well as report out useful
campaign-related information.

o *Fundraising and Audio Presentations:* Prepare materials and presentations for potential major donors and volunteers as the campaign progresses.

o *Foundation Research and Proposals:* Identify, research and prepare letters of inquiry or formal grant requests to selected foundations ensuring personal follow-up to encourage favorable consideration, or in the event of a grant declination, request helpful suggestions for future submissions.

o *Campaign Events: Planning and Implementation:* Plan the logistical requirements for special events such as a campaign "kick-off", major donor cultivation, volunteer "rallies", ground breaking ceremonies, campaign conclusion celebration.

o *Volunteer Leadership, Staff and Support:* Ensure sufficient professional staff time and skills are available to support gift solicitations and volunteer involvement.

* * *

The next page illustrates the key management and support functions.

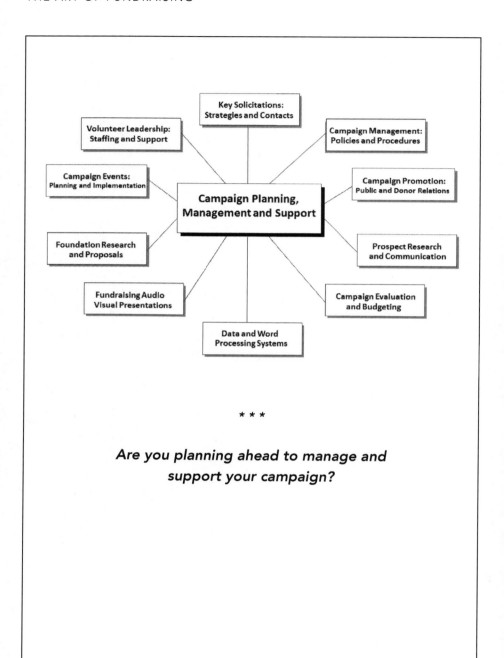

Key Solicitations:
Strategies and Contacts

Volunteer Leadership:
Staffing and Support

Campaign Management:
Policies and Procedures

Campaign Events:
Planning and Implementation

Campaign Promotion:
Public and Donor Relations

Campaign Planning,
Management and Support

Foundation Research
and Proposals

Prospect Research
and Communication

Fundraising Audio
Visual Presentations

Campaign Evaluation
and Budgeting

Data and Word
Processing Systems

\* \* \*

*Are you planning ahead to manage and
support your campaign?*

# THE STRATEGIES

Successful fundraising depends on thoughtful application of sound strategies in communicating an organization's compelling case to potential donors. Strategies such as encouraging endowment gifts; integrating annual giving into capital campaigns; funding campaign costs; and assessing fundraising effectiveness.

# Campaign Gift Models

Many non-profits treat Campaign Gift Models as perfunctory exercises, constructed before the real business of raising money gets underway. But when thoughtfully developed and periodically reviewed, a Campaign Gift Model can be an indispensable tool in both planning and assessing the progress of major fundraising campaigns.

The following list highlights areas that model metrics can help design a campaign and measure results. The terms in bold italics represent column headings in the Campaign Gift Model illustrated below.

***Prospective Donors***: Projects the number of *prospects required* as compared to current *prospects identified* within suggested dollar "target" ranges.

***Campaign Feasibility***: Gains a preliminary assessment of a campaign's potential success based on *projected dollars* from current *prospects identified.*

**Campaign Phasing**: Can help gauge phasing of a campaign based on number of _prospects required_ to meet sequential dollar goal objectives; for example: silent, leadership, major and general gift solicitation phases.

**Campaign Materials**: Helps to estimate the number and nature of printed materials and visual presentations required during each phase of the campaign based on number of _prospects required_ to be engaged.

**Campaign Volunteers:** Can be used to estimate the number and capability of volunteers to engage in personal contact with _prospects required_ in each phase of the campaign.

**"Naming" Opportunities**: Assists in identifying specific opportunities, based on _donors required_ within indicated top _gift ranges,_ to "name" major facilities and features of project(s) to be funded through the campaign.

**Campaign Honor Roll**: Can help determine categories of donors to be honored within selected _gift ranges_ at the conclusion of the campaign.

**Campaign Staff and Budget**: Aids in projecting fundraising staff and allocating budgeted resources to each campaign phase based on reasonable expectations for cost/result fundraising effectiveness.

*Campaign Mid-Course Evaluations*: Provides guidelines for assessing campaign progress for possible mid-course corrections when comparing Campaign Gift Model projections to campaign results to date.

| 10 MILLION CAMPAIGN GIFT MODEL | | | | CURRENT PROSPECTS | |
|---|---|---|---|---|---|
| GIFT RANGES | DONORS REQUIRED | PROSPECTS REQUIRED | DOLLARS | PROSPECTS IDENTIFIED | PROJECTED DOLLARS |
| $2 million + | 1 | 2 | $2,000,000 | | |
| $1 million + | 2 | 4 | $2,000,000 | | |
| $500,000 + | 2 | 4 | $1,000,000 | | |
| $250,000 + | 4 | 8 | $1,000,000 | | |
| $100,000 + | 10 | 30 | $1,000,000 | | |
| $50,000 + | 20 | 60 | $1,000,000 | | |
| $25,000 + | 40 | 120 | $1,000,000 | | |
| $10,000 + | 50 | 150 | $500,000 | | |
| Less than $10,000 | many | many | $500,000 | | |
| Total | 129+ | 378+ | $10,000000 | | |

An organization can fill out the last two columns – *Prospects Identified* and *Projected Dollars* –based on its retained donor data base and knowledge of potential donors, particularly at the highest projected gift ranges or results from a Campaign Feasibility Study. Given these projections, an organization can get an early assessment of campaign potential and decide on next steps.

\* \* \*

*Has your organization modeled its approach to a successful major fundraising campaign?*

# Integrating Annual Giving in a Capital Campaign

For a vast majority of non-profit organizations, annual giving is the "life blood" of operations, providing a flow of indispensable income to support ongoing programs and activities. When contemplating a major fundraising campaign, questions inevitably arise about how to not disrupt the flow of annual gifts while simultaneously soliciting campaign gifts.

The following strategies can be applied individually as well as in combination to minimize negative impact on annual giving during a capital campaign.

o  ***Clarity of Purpose:*** Communicate in advance as well as during the campaign the essential and distinctive purposes of both annual giving and the capital campaign, i.e. annual giving sustains ongoing operations, and campaign giving funds opportunities to enhance physical facilities and add to endowment.

o  ***"Over and Above" Gifts:*** Request that donors' consider capital campaign gifts "over and above" their customary or intended annual gifts. This approach is most effective during early major gift solicitations and can be reinforced with donor recognition opportunities for both annual and campaign donors.

o **_Early Solicitation of Major Gifts:_** Focus early in the campaign on personal solicitation of individuals who have the greatest financial capacity. This can be followed in subsequent years by solicitation of their ongoing annual support.

o **_General Campaign:_** When 75 percent to 90 percent of the campaign dollar goal has been achieved, broaden solicitation to the entire constituency through the use of direct mail, telephone follow-up, general constituency communications and special events. At this point, some organizations combine annual and campaign giving for a specific period to simplify donor decisions as suggested in _Distinctive Donor Recognition_ below. An alternative would be to solicit campaign gifts during the first six months of the year and annual gifts during the last six months.

o **_Distinctive Donor Recognition:_** During the final phase of the campaign the entire constituency is solicited for a combined annual and campaign gift in order to simplify donor decisions, maximize gift support, and encourage repeat gifts from early major donors. For example, for the final six months campaign gifts at specified levels, e.g. $500, $1,000, $2,000, $5,000, will come with distinctive donor recognition for both annual and campaign support.

\* \* \*

***What will be your organization's approach to annual giving during a capital campaign?***

# Campaign Feasibility Studies

Often considered no more than a tool to determine whether or not to embark on an intended capital campaign, well-designed campaign feasibility studies help to determine realistic goals as well as specific ways to increase an organization's fundraising effectiveness and results. Candid comments and appraisals from potential major donors and volunteer leaders offer valued insights into planning a successful fundraising campaign. Both the value and validity of this advance assessment is dependent, in large measure, on thoughtful and thorough preparation in the following key areas.

## Preliminary Campaign Case

First and foremost, a concise and clearly articulated statement of the essential rationale needs to be developed with projected costs for funding proposed new buildings, facility renovations, endowment, and major programs. This initial "test" case eventually will be refined to reflect candid observations of individuals interviewed during the study.

## Interviewees

Individuals to be personally interviewed should be identified based on the following judged characteristics:

o *prior involvement with/expressed interest in the organization and its fundamental mission;*

o *financial capacity to make a major gift commitment in an anticipated capital campaign;*

o *ability and willingness to persuade others to support the organization and its funding objectives;*

o *prominence in business, civic and/or philanthropic leadership.*

## Budgetary Commitment

Following the Feasibility Study the organization's leadership needs to ensure that sufficient budget can be made available to carry-out a recommended action plan which may include adding professional fundraising staff and/or campaign counsel, campaign materials and presentations, as well as campaign data base management.

*  *  *

*Is your organization planning a comprehensive campaign feasibility to launch rather than lurch into a capital campaign?*

# Feasibility Studies: Getting Answers

While methodologies may vary in conducting campaign feasibility studies, comprehensive and reliable study results should respond to the following questions:

1. *What is the potential for the organization to raise private contributions and grants necessary to fund identified facilities and programs described in the Funding Prospectus?*

2. *How can the organization most effectively engage leadership in the early planning stages of a major fundraising campaign?*

3. *What are the most persuasive and compelling reasons the organization can offer to potential major donors to encourage their support?*

4. *What do the organization's friends and supporters think about its current fundraising, i.e. strengths and weaknesses?*

5. Does the organization have a sufficient number of potential major donors for a successful major fundraising campaign?

6. What is the organization's best overall strategy to reach an ambitious but realistic campaign dollar goal in the shortest period of time?

7. What are expectations of the organization's Board and staff in achieving a successful campaign?

8. Who should be asked to take on volunteer leadership of the organization's campaign?

9. How much will a major fundraising campaign cost, and what are some ways the organization might consider in funding these costs?

10. How can the organization most effectively sustain ongoing annual fundraising during a major fundraising campaign?

* * *

**Are these questions being considered by your organization when contemplating a campaign?**

# Funding Campaign Expenses

There are various approaches to cover campaign fundraising expenses until adequate cash is received from pledged commitments. An organization can use the following techniques either independently or combined, depending on their financial resources and campaign dollar goals.

- o *Annual Operating Budget:* Early campaign expenses can be covered by the organization's annual operating budget until sufficient unrestricted funds are received from donors.

- o *Board Campaign Fund:* Board members' early campaign cash contributions are pooled to cover initial campaign expenses. If requested, these funds can be replenished for subsequent designated purposes as unrestricted cash gifts are received from other donors.

- o *Endowment Borrowing:* The organization's endowment can loan funds that are repaid, often at or below prime rate interest, as unrestricted cash gifts are received from donors.

o **Allocation from Contributions:** A percentage from all cash contributions, for example 10 percent, is allocated to fund campaign expenses throughout the course of the campaign. This allocation may be used to: a) replenish the Board Campaign Fund, b) repay the Endowment, and/or c) cover subsequent campaign expenses. Any excess in allocated funds can be reallocated at the conclusion of the campaign to meet the campaign's featured funding objectives.

A couple of related points:

o *Campaign budgeted expenses should be integrated into the campaign's total dollar goal so that these costs can be recouped.*

o *As a budgeting guideline, campaign expenses generally range from 5 percent to 15 percent of the total campaign dollar goal.*

o *In developing a campaign budget, personnel costs will likely be between 60 percent and 65 percent of all campaign budgeted expenditures.*

\* \* \*

**How is your organization budgeting and covering campaign expenditures?**

# Guidelines for Assessing Fundraising Cost/Result Effectiveness

Far too many non-profit organizations fail to assess their fundraising effectiveness in terms of the relationship between direct costs and resulting donations. The following guidelines can be helpful in making such assessments, but keep in mind that many variables – from organization size and geographic location, to mission and special programs – have to be taken into consideration when making a final judgment about fundraising effectiveness.

## Overall Cost/Result Effectiveness

Generally speaking, a range of 15 percent to 25 percent of direct costs to dollars raised is a good guideline for most non-profit organizations involved in comprehensive fund- and friend-raising efforts. Fundraising includes all efforts and activities by an organization to secure charitable contributions. Friend-raising focuses on constituency-relation programs sustained through publications, communications, and special events. The percentages above are just guidelines: spending less than 15 percent may represent an under-investment in fundraising, while for some organizations, spending more than 25 percent over the near term may represent wise investment in new fundraising programs and initiatives.

# Fundraising Methodologies: Cost/Result Effectiveness

*Direct Response Marketing*: A 35 percent to 100 percent ratio of direct costs to dollars raised is a broad guideline for direct mail and telemarketing fundraising. Ratios in the higher range typically result from new donor acquisition efforts. When soliciting an identified, well-informed constituency, such as an alumni body, ratios in the 15 percent to 35 percent range can be achieved. The major costs of direct response marketing generally involve the design, printing and distribution of fundraising materials, and, if utilized, the services of a reputable telemarketing firm.

*Major Gifts Solicitations:* A 5 percent to 15 percent ratio of direct costs to dollars raised can be achieved through the process of personal contact, cultivation and solicitation of potential major donors, especially when both dedicated volunteers and experienced professional staff are involved. The direct costs would include professional staff time along with personalized solicitation materials and presentations.

*Capital and Endowment Campaigns*: A 5 percent to 15 percent ratio is a reasonable guideline for major fundraising campaigns focused on securing a number of high-end initial "transformational" and "lead" gifts. Such campaigns would commonly progress through sequential phases of solicitation from higher to lower dollar gift levels, with a final phase of broad solicitation efforts typically utilizing direct response marketing.

*Special Events*: An inaugural fundraising special event may yield disappointing fundraising results after considering the initial start-up and operating costs involved as well the inevitable "lessons learned" to be corrected in future events. Over subsequent years, however, 50 percent to 80 percent of event net proceeds from gross revenues may be an achievable goal.

*Website*: Reliable statistics of cost/result effectiveness from web-based fundraising is not yet available.

* * *

*How is your organization assessing its fundraising cost/result effectiveness?*

# When Do We Go Public?

I am frequently asked by staff and volunteers *"when do we go public"* with their campaign. My response is to provide the following general guidelines:

### 'Quiet Phase'

As the initial phase of a campaign, generally 12 months to 24 months in duration, the objective is to focus on securing gift commitments from donors most intimately involved with the institution. An objective is to demonstrate that the campaign will be ultimately successful in order to eventually encourage donors beyond the intimate group to join in the effort.

Often a *'working campaign goal'* is established for the *'Quiet Phase'* with gift results aiding the institution to establish a realistic campaign dollar goal prior to launching the *'Public Phase'*.

Gift objectives during the *Quiet Phase* generally are to secure gift commitments toward the initial "working goal" with:

o   a "lead" gift commitment representing 15% to 20% of the campaign dollar goal;

o   100% gift participation from the governing board totaling from 10% to 30% of the campaign dollar goal;

o   several major gifts, which together with a "lead" and governing board gifts, should total between 60% to 80% of the campaign dollar goal.

During the 'Quiet 'Phase many of the institution's supporters and friends, and certainly those people being solicited, will be well aware that a campaign is underway, so terms like "quiet" and "silent" are a bit misleading.

Based essentially on the magnitude of the campaign dollar goal as well as the size and geographical distribution of an institution's constituency, one of two intermediate campaign phases may be planned before entering into the 'Public Phase'.

**'Public Phase'**

When the campaign approaches 70% to 80% of the represented dollar goal through focused major gift solicitations, it will be time to consider more broadly communicating the campaign's funding goals and success to date. Communicating more broadly to your organization's entire data base constituency, the general public, and potential donors who have to date declined or neglected to make a campaign gift commitment.

Moving into a public phase too early can result in more modest gift commitments from potential major donors before you have an opportunity to personally contact, communicate and convince them to become major donors.

\* \* \*

***What is your organization's policy regarding commencement of construction for new facilities?***

# When Do We Break Ground?

During most capital campaigns there comes a time when a few major donors and volunteer leaders may press earnestly for commencement of construction of the featured buildings and facilities. While well-intended, this pressure too often overlooks the related costs of *"financing the delta"*, i.e. borrowing cash required, over and above cash gifts received and pledge payments due, to pay for construction, furnishings, equipping the building and surrounding landscaping.

A wise institutional policy is to establish *before* a campaign is launched, and *before* predictable impatience leads to imprudent financial decisions–specific criteria for commencement of construction. The criteria to be applied in such a policy will vary based on an organization's access to construction funding and financing; consideration of escalating construction costs; and, revenue generating aspects of the new building and facilities.

For example, a policy guideline to consider is:

*Construction of the campaign's featured building objectives will commence when no less than 70 percent of the total costs of the project has been received in cash and confirmed cash pledges, and with no less than 30 percent received in cash and with pledge payments due within 3 years from commencement of construction.*

Organizations are wise to be cautious of tax-exempt bond issuances and other sources of financing for worthy projects. The amortization costs of such financing to hasten completion of promised buildings which may bear a donor's name will be borne by future generations of governing Boards, donors and development officers.

\* \* \*

**What is your organization's policy to protect against premature decisions to commence construction?**

# Funding Donor-Initiated Projects

Let's presume you work with an organization that takes a thoughtful and measured approach to its capital projects. First, a comprehensive Master Plan for capital projects has been developed in consultation and rigorous planning with experts in the fields of architecture, site development, and construction. Next, your Board assigns priorities to capital projects to ensure important initiatives identified through master planning will be funded in a logical sequence. You are all set to proceed, or are well into an intensive capital campaign when reality arrives from the philanthropic marketplace!

From time to time a potential major donor may wish to give and raise funds for facilities or projects in advance, or even outside the scope of Board-determined funding priorities. While non-profit organizations welcome support it is advisable that policies be established in advance to avoid potential conflicts with enthusiastic donors. With that in mind, the following guidelines should be considered by the governing Board.

> **Master Plan Facility or Project**: A facility or project must be included within, or formally added to the organization's Board approved Master Plan.

*Approved Total Estimated Costs:* The estimated "hard" and "soft" costs of the project along with the assumptions used in estimating these costs must be reviewed and approved by the Board.

*Confirmed "Lead" Gift Commitment:* A single donor must confirm both willingness and ability to contribute no less than 50 percent of the total estimated costs, with a pledged commitment payable over no more than 3 years.

*Approved Potential Donors:* A list of potential donors to the project must be reviewed and approved by the Board in order to avoid significant conflicts with the organization's ongoing fundraising efforts.

*Commencement of Facility Construction or Project Initiation:* Commencement of facility construction or project initiation will follow assurances that no less than 90 percent of the approved estimated project costs have been secured.

* * *

*What are your organization's guidelines for funding donor-initiated projects?*

# Naming a Building

There are a number of things to consider when a non-profit organization seeks or is offered an opportunity to "name" a new or existing building in return for a donor's generous gift commitment. A key consideration is that a naming gift does not represent a donor's ownership interest in the building, new or existing, but rather provides the institution a distinctive opportunity to honor the donor/donor family in a special way.

## Organizational Considerations

### Gift Level

Many large organizations set a naming gift level at 50 percent of the cost of a building as a starting point for discussions with potential major donors. While organizations may establish a lesser gift level these "naming" gift levels tend to set both the standards and expectations for other prominent recognition opportunities. For example, if an organization accepts a $1 million gift to name a building costing $10 million, it may be difficult to

THE ART OF FUNDRAISING

establish meaningful recognition for other major donors to secure the balance of $9 million.

**Cash Commitment**

For building construction or major renovation, the availability of cash is an important consideration. If less cash is available early in the construction process the result can be higher interest costs for external financing or operating budget pressures. While a 10-year cash pledge to name a building may be a thoughtful gift, it is likely to put the institution in a difficult cash position. Generally, a three- to five-year pledge is sought for a naming gift commitment. Obviously, pledge terms will be based on consideration of a donor's charitable intentions and financial circumstances.

**"Packaged" Gift Commitments**

Sometimes a donor will offer a gift commitment of a cash pledge with initial cash payment along with an irrevocable estate planned gift, or another valued asset such as real estate. In these cases, an organization's clearly articulated gift acceptance policies covering gifts of cash and cash-equivalents such as real estate and estate planned gifts are essential in judging both acceptability and intrinsic value of such a gift.

## Consideration of the Details

Well-intentioned gift commitments to name a building can become problematic over time as a result of inattention to details during gift negotiations. If, in the future - for example after 35 years - the building requires major renovation or demolition, the organization will need a policy in place at the time of the confirmed gift commitment to address these circumstances. Options include honoring donor names with a permanent plaque at the new site, or giving the donor/donor family the opportunity to renew a financial commitment to name the new or renovated building.

In addition, in negotiating the terms and conditions of a naming gift, special ticketing, seating, parking privileges and other such perquisites distinctive to the organization are often as important to a wealthy donor and family as is naming of the building.

With such considerations in mind, the most important thing to remember is that the donor's interests, concerns, wishes and conditions of their naming gift commitment will be revealed through thoughtful discussions and negotiations.

* * *

***Are you prepared to enter into discussions with a wealthy donor to "name" a building?***

# Fundraising in Difficult Economic Times

Our nation periodically faces difficult economic times, which is subsequently imposed on our non-profit organizations. Gifts from every stratum of donors may decline as lower income families struggle to make ends meet and middle class households get by on less disposable income. Wealthy individuals become extra cautious in considering sizable gifts from their accumulated assets, often resulting in extended and complex gift negotiations.

But an even bigger concern confronting fundraising during difficult economic times is an often diminishing level of effort, enthusiasm, and energy from non-profits to compete more effectively for available financial resources and volunteer leadership. Organizations may presume that economic circumstances beyond their control justify cutting budgets with little concurrent effort to increase revenues. Board members withdrawing from earnest fundraising, and reducing their previous level of gift commitments. Professional staff moving from major gift efforts to work on special events favoured by well-meaning volunteers.

What needed during difficult economic times is a "back to basics" approach, one that relies on the three essential elements of effective fundraising: case, constituency, and leadership.

*Case:* The ability to articulate in a compelling, consistent and confident manner the organization's fundamental merit and pressing financial needs which fundamentally translate into helping others; helping through education, health and human services, youth development.

*Constituency:* The capacity to communicate directly and as personally as possible with a substantial number of individuals judged most likely to become donors, supporters and advocates for the organization.

*Leadership:* Top volunteer and staff leadership who inspire both confidence and effort in those around them and secure support for the organization.

A punctuation point: strong organizational leadership is the absolute key. Strong leadership can often overcome a less than adequate case. Strong leadership can frequently assist in developing an expanded constituency. However, without strong leadership an organization may be left without the ability to effectively compete for people's time, attention and resources.

\* \* \*

***How effectively is your organization competing for peoples' time, attention and resources?***

# ENDOWMENT

*"A goal without a plan is just a wish"*

Most non-profit organizations admit to needing endowment, most often with no plan or sustained effort to achieve realistic endowment goals. Planning and sustaining efforts to raise endowment is just as strategic for an organization's future financial sustainability as seeking current expendable funding.

# Eliminating Debt

Unfortunately, a growing number of non-profit organizations are finding themselves burdened with debt most often resulting from expansion of facilities, programs, and services during optimistic economic times. When debt repayment becomes burdensome to operating budgets, organizations are faced with the challenge of attempting to persuade major donors to help eliminate that debt. Not a very compelling case for support, but nevertheless a case that might be made in the following manner.

## Balance Sheet Initiative

One way to make the case for gifts to reduce debt is a *Balance Sheet Initiative*, a fundraising theme in which the organization asks potential major donors to aid in securing all buildings and grounds "free and clear" on the organization's balance sheet. Donors can be attracted to this initiative because it will enable the organization to redirect related annual principal and interest payments to its fundamental mission: serving people and the community.

In building this case, it is important to communicate to potential major donors that a gift to the *Balance Sheet Initiative* is essentially equivalent to gifts to endowment. For example:

**Debt Principal and Interest**: An organization currently carries external debt of $5 million with annual principal and interest payments totalling $500,000.

**Equivalent Endowment**: With $5 million in gifts to pay this debt in full, the organization would be relieved of $500,000 in annual principal and interest payments. Those funds could then be redirected for undesignated or donor designated purposes within the organization's annual operating budget. The total of these gifts would represent the equivalent of a $10 million in permanent endowment, generating $500,000 per year for the annual operating budget based on a 5 percent rate of return.

**Special Donor Recognition**: A donor of an equivalent endowment gift could be recognized both annually at the level of his/her/their pledge payments as well as permanently as an "endower" of the organization.

\* \* \*

*How is your organization handling its debt financing?*

# Another Look at Endowment

The essential importance of endowment is that it is a reliable source of predictable income enabling an organization to meet its previous commitments made to people in providing services, employment and financial assurances.

Securing and growing a sizeable permanent endowment is a goal for most non-profit organizations. However, for many donors an endowment gift may seem like a significant financial investment with limited current financial impact, falling well-short of their goal to provide *meaningful* financial support. In light of that, donors may appreciate having the option of giving a present-term endowment providing a specified annual dollar distribution, in contrast to permanent endowment that provides a specified annual income distribution.

o **Permanent Endowment:** A $1 million gift for permanent endowment that generates five percent in annual income will provide $50,000 each year to meet the expressed needs of the organization along with the wishes of the donor.

THE ART OF FUNDRAISING

o **Present-Term Endowment:** A $1 million gift for present-term endowment provides $100,000 in annual income, but would require invading endowment principal to add to generated annual income. This would likely deplete the endowment within 15 years based on a five percent average return on retained funds.

There are several factors to consider in deciding whether a present-term endowment gift would be valued by both the donor and the organization. Depleting present-term endowment dedicated to an ongoing financial need would require fundraising at some point in time to replenish the principal. As an alternative to depleting the funds, the originating donor might consider a collateral bequest to secure the permanency of the endowment.

An additional factor to consider in soliciting endowment gifts is that some major donors may express reluctance to provide permanent endowment because it could eliminate the need for an organization to be continuously accountable to its donors, i.e. its "investors".

* * *

**Would a present-term endowment be an option your donors might value?**

# Encouraging Cash Endowment Gifts

Most, if not all, charitable organizations strive to build up cash in their endowment in order to secure a reliable source of predictable income. Most major donors–but fortunately *not* all–are reluctant to donate cash for endowment which will only enable their recipient charity to spend roughly five percent per year.

"I'll keep the principal and donate the interest annually!" donors sometimes express.

The problem, of course, is that non-profit organizations have ongoing financial commitments requiring a reasonably predictable income. These commitments include those that support a vision and a mission—educating the young, feeding the hungry, making the community healthier — as well as day-to-day financial commitments that impact peoples' lives, such as students' financial aid checks, purchasing food, and paying salaries of scientific researchers, child care workers, or nurses. A prudent organization needs to have secure sources of reliable income in order to make such commitments to people. While donor intentions to provide annual gifts rather than endowment are honorable, their financial circumstances may change in later years and hinder their ability to make those annual gifts.

Here are some suggestions to help persuade a donor questioning whether or not to keep his/her principal and donate the annual income:

o *Emphasize Value Added:* Donors are often persuaded to make a gift if the organization can clearly articulate how the increased endowment will provide added value, i.e. help the organization to accomplish more....achieve better results...keep a program that might otherwise be cut. Not merely to provide more income for the general operating budget, but to provide added value for the both the donor and the organization.

o *Identify End-Use:* Donors often give from a sense of urgency when they understand the potential impact on people's lives. When the organization articulates beyond the general value added from endowment income the specifics related to the number and circumstances of people served... more...better... are not to be overlooked.

o *Meaningful Naming Opportunities:* In my years in philanthropy I have met very few anonymous donors. Most people like to have their names associated with worthy, highly-regarded organizations. Endowed funds named to honor donors can be established to encourage donors to contribute the necessary assets for an endowment, or, for example, *The John Smith Family Fund for Neo-Natal Care* to purchase the latest in technological advancements; *The John Smith Financial Aid Fund* for students selecting the sciences for their course of study; *The John and Judy Smith Fund* for art classes in designated socio-economic areas.

* * *

**How is your organization encouraging cash gifts to endowment?**

# Borrowing and Accessing Endowment

When adopting policies which define and restrict the use of endowment, governing Boards need to be mindful of the future. Not just what present day circumstances may dictate, but those unforeseen challenges others might face in years to come. What if the organization faces a serious future financial crisis that could be solved by accessing cash in its endowment? Who can foretell when the financing of major facility renovations could strain the operating budget?

Unlike most other governing Board actions which can be reversed or amended, policies defining and restricting endowment funds are a covenant with donors. Lifting those restrictions in the future can be difficult to do.

## Borrowing Endowment

Non-profits organizations should consider policies which would enable it to borrow funds from its endowment under a specific set of provisions such as:

o   *requiring majority approval by the then-serving Board;*

o   *not exceeding a certain percentage of endowment principal, e.g. 25 percent ;*

o   *adopting a repayment schedule over no more than five years with interest at the then current prime interest rate.*

## Accessing Endowment

Non-profits should consider a policy that would permit accessing endowment funds under a specific set of conditions such as:

o   *requiring unanimous approval of the then serving governing Board;*

o   *not exceeding a certain percentage of endowment principal., e.g. 15 percent;*

Any new policies for borrowing or accessing endowment would not be easily applied retroactively without individual donor consent, and should not be applied to endowed funds where income has been designated by donors for specific expenditure purposes.

In advising endowment donors of such policies, consideration should be given to satisfying donor wishes and intentions with the possibility of making appropriate policy exceptions as judged necessary in the best interests of both the organization and donor.

* * *

*What are your organization's policies for borrowing and accessing endowment funds?*

# Should We Include Endowment in Our Capital Campaign?

Non-profit organizations often are in a quandary as to whether they should increase their capital campaign dollar goals to include endowment sufficient to cover projected increases in annual operating costs for new or renovated facilities. It can be a tough decision, made tougher by the different perspectives of the stakeholders who are involved in that decision making process. Here are several perspectives heard from our firm's clients:

## From a Principal Donor's perspective…

*"I want to be assured that the building to be named for my family as a result of our contribution will be properly maintained and operated over the years. I don't want the carpets to get frayed …. or the paint to peel…or programs eliminated because of budget cuts. I want the campaign to raise an endowment for the building to cover those costs."*

## From a Financial Officer's perspective...

*"I shudder to think of covering the increase in our annual operating costs for the upkeep, maintenance, and programming of the new building without an added endowment. That definitely needs to be a fundraising goal of the campaign."*

## From a Board Member's perspective....

*"It will be tough enough to raise funds to build this building. Let's not overburden our fundraising by including endowment in our campaign goal. We can leave that until later...and for others to deal with."*

## From a Senior Executive's perspective...

*"Even though I'm very concerned about the added operating costs we'll face, I don't want to stand in the way of the Board's efforts to 'get the job done' as quickly as possible. Rather than attempt to raise endowment now, I guess we'll just have to increase our annual giving to cover the costs."*

## From a Development Officer's perspective...

*"I'm going to have a difficult enough time raising the cash required to pay for this construction project. Frankly, I'd just as soon not be asked to simultaneously raise funds for endowment."*

In response to these divergent stakeholder views, an organization could consider the following course of action:

o *Include a specific endowment dollar goal in the campaign with the provision that any "fall short" at the conclusion of the campaign will be rolled into an ongoing endowment fundraising effort supported by dedicated volunteers and professional staff.*

o *Provide distinctive donor recognition opportunities for endowment donors.*

o *Emphasize opportunities for estate planned gifts.*

Based on an organization's circumstances I have also suggested that a fixed percentage of all campaign gifts, for example, 10 percent, be allocated to endowment. This provision needs to be communicated to donors.

* * *

**How will your organization provide for an endowment fundraising goal in your campaign?**

# GENERAL

Following are some general thoughts and suggestions I wanted to share with you.

# Puns From The Podium

You likely have, and will be asked to make a presentation. It's often a good idea to begin or interject in your presentation some light-hearted remarks which serve to both relax your audience... as well as yourself. Here are some to consider.

Paraprosdokians are figures of speech in which the latter part of a sentence or phrase is surprising or unexpected.

o   Where there's a will, I want to be in it.

o   Knowledge is knowing a tomato is a fruit. Wisdom is not putting it in a fruit salad.

o   An expert designed the Titanic. An amateur designed the Ark.

o   To steal ideas from one person is plagiarism. To steal from many is research.

o   I didn't say it was your fault, I said I was blaming you.

- o You do not need a parachute to skydive. You only need a parachute to skydive twice.

- o To be sure of hitting the target, shoot first and call whatever you hit the target.

- o Going to church doesn't make you a Christian any more than standing in a garage makes you a car.

- o I'm supposed to respect my elders, but it's getting harder and harder for me to find one now.

A potpourri of puns

- o Change is inevitable, except from a vending machine.

- o All those who believe in psycho kinesis, raise my hand.

- o The early bird catches the worm, but the second mouse gets the cheese.

- o The only substitute for bad manners is fast reflexes.

- o I changed my password to "*incorrect*", so whenever I forget it the computer will say, "*Your password is incorrect*".

- o Everyone has a photographic memory. Some people just don't have film.

# Eleemosynary Environmentalists

*Eleemosynary Environmentalist: (n.) A person dedicated to protecting one of our nation's most endangered species, the fundraising volunteer.*

The fundraising profession attracts some of the world's finest people, dedicated to the worthiest of causes that vitalize our unique philanthropic tradition. Preserving that philanthropic tradition requires that today's non-profit sector professionals become eleemosynary environmentalists, committed to preserving and protecting the increasingly elusive and endangered fundraising volunteer!

With dramatic growth in our nation's non-profit sector, we are facing a dwindling supply of men and women who are able and willing to volunteer their time to persuade others to support their chosen charitable institutions. Major fundraising campaigns for universities and cultural institutions are concluding with dollar goals reached but with short rosters of fundraising volunteers to thank. Charitable organizations dedicated to community health, youth and welfare are struggling to enlist volunteers to aid them in securing gifts and grants.

Our profession needs to renew a once-vigorous commitment to volunteers. We must enlist and encourage their efforts. Be patient when their good intentions don't translate into immediate results. Shelter them from ill–defined responsibilities and incomplete planning. Refrain from giving them tasks better suited for professionals, such as preparing organizational plans, materials and events.

The highest and best use of volunteers is to have them encourage and solicit support from others. It is our responsibility to preserve their essential role as "rain-makers" in philanthropy. Perhaps a theme for our renewed professional commitment to volunteer fundraisers should be: Accentuate the asking, and eliminate the elementary.

As with the whales, condors and our world's rain forests, we need to protect and care for fundraising volunteers. Without them, organizations dedicated to the arts, education and public service have little chance of meeting the challenges to their financial survival. The time has come for all of us to become eleemosynary environmentalists.

* * *

**What are you doing to preserve your volunteer resources?**

# Institutional Integrity

From time to time a potential significant donor may wish to give as well as raise funds for something in which they are especially interested, but which may not be within an organization's defined master plan or funding priorities. And their philanthropic interests may translate into related specifications and requirements which may not be in the organization's best interests...potentially jeopardizing its "institutional integrity".

In the spirit of encouraging rather than discouraging welcomed financial support, I recommend that our clients consider policy guidelines which aid in protecting their organization's institutional integrity. The following is an example of such a policy guideline.

* * *

*Prior to authorizing our organization's commitment to fund a specific project, program or facility not currently within the approved master plan or operational funding priorities the following guidelines will be applied.*

*Master Plan/Funding Priorities:* The governing Board must formally approve the proposed project, program or facility to be integrated within the organization's current master plan and operational plan.

*Approved Estimated Costs:* The estimated "hard" and "soft" costs along with the assumptions used in estimating these costs must be reviewed and approved by the governing board.

- o *Confirmed "Lead" Gift Commitment:* A single donor must confirm both willingness and ability to contribute no less than 50% of the total estimated costs, with a written pledged commitment payable over no more than 3 years.

- o *Approved Potential Donors:* When funding will be required from additional donors a list of those potential donors will be reviewed and approved by the governing board in order to avoid significant conflicts with the organization's ongoing fundraising efforts and activities.

- o *Commencement of Project, Program or Facility:* Commencement of the specified project, program or facility will follow confirmation that no less than 90% of the approved estimated costs have been secured.

o *Funding Terms and Conditions:* Terms and conditions of a significant gift commitment which specifies donor(s) "naming" privilege and expenditure requirements as well as other key considerations will require governing board approval.

As with any major financial transaction these guidelines provide a point-of-departure for thoughtful discussions and negotiations to ensure a donor's best interests as well as the organization's institutional integrity are kept upper most in mind.

# Ethical Conduct…Who Judges?

Professionals in philanthropy are occasionally presented with circumstances in which their decisions have ethical implications. For example, how would you respond to the following?

o   Is it ethical to accept a "gratuity" from a donor in return for helping to negotiate complex terms and conditions for a major gift that provided the donor with special recognition such as "naming" a building?

o   Is it ethical to accept from an estate planned gift donor a bequest to you in appreciation for your assistance in attending to the final philanthropic wishes of his now deceased wife?

o   Is it ethical to accept from a "booster" an all-expense paid weekend vacation at his beach front condo, traveling on his private jet, after you were able to legitimately provide him with much sought after season tickets?

Who judges the ethical implications of your decision? You, based on your personal integrity? Your non-profit organization, which likely has policies in place with respect to such circumstances? A professional association, in which you or your organization are members? The answer is most likely all of the above.

But not to be overlooked is the judgment of the general public your organization serves as a result of being granted tax-exempt status. Keeping that in mind, when faced with a decision which may involve ethical considerations a good test question is: *"If I make this decision could it result in an investigative reporters headline in our local newspaper or on the evening news?"* Decisions which may impinge on ethical conduct should be considered from the perspective of all involved parties: the individual; his/her organization; related professional association; and, most importantly, the public served.

95371304R00095

Made in the USA
San Bernardino, CA
15 November 2018